## Finding the Funny in Hot Flashes, Mood Swings and the Mystery Chin Hairs

**ANGELIQUEA PASSAGLIA**

*Jumpstart*
PUBLISHING

Copyright © 2025 by Angeliquea Passaglia and Passaglia Insurance Agency Inc. All rights reserved. No part of this book or its associated ancillary materials may be reproduced or transmitted in any form or by any means, electronic or mechanical, including photocopying, recording, or by any informational storage or retrieval system without permission from the author or publisher. Connect with the author at www.AngeliqueaPassaglia.com.

Published by Jumpstart Publishing, PO Box 6, Roseville, CA 95661. (916) 872-4000 www.JumpstartPublishing.net

**DISCLAIMER AND/OR LEGAL NOTICES**

While all attempts have been made to verify information provided in this book and its ancillary materials, neither the author or publisher assumes any responsibility for errors, inaccuracies, or omissions and is not responsible for any loss by customer in any manner. Any slights of people or organizations are unintentional. This book and its associated ancillary materials, including verbal and written training, is not intended for use as a source of personal or medical advice.

ISBN: 979-8-218-64111-5

Printed in the United States

# DEDICATION

This book is dedicated to my Momma, my built-in best friend and one-lady cheering squad.

To all my gal pals and Shelli Tierney-Berg—
I miss you every day, and I so wish you were going through all of this with me, mostly for the laughs!

To Mercedes, thank you for all our late-night brainstorming sessions.

To Jordan, you are my forever rooster and spirit human.

And to my husband, Michael, thank you for putting up with my menopause and encouraging me to complete this book and believing in me. You are definitely my biggest fan. I love you more than words could ever express. You will always be my wonder twin.

I also want to thank Katrina Sawa, without you this would still be in my computer.

And thank you to Kristen Hugins for your magic.

# TABLE OF CONTENTS

**INTRODUCTION** ............................................................... 1

**CHAPTER 1**
    WHERE DID MY PERIOD GO? .................................3

**CHAPTER 2**
    WOW! I AM SO HOT! ................................................11

**CHAPTER 3**
    WEIGHT GAIN ............................................................19

**CHAPTER 4**
    LET'S TALK ABOUT SEX ...........................................27

**CHAPTER 5**
    TO BOTOX OR NOT TO BOTOX? ...........................37

**CHAPTER 6**
    OUR VAGINA ..............................................................53

**CHAPTER 7**

    SLEEP, BRAIN FOG, LACK OF ENERGY, MOOD SWINGS .................................................................. 63

**CHAPTER 8**

    I COULD CARE LESS! ................................................. 71

**CHAPTER 9**

    MAN-ON-PAUSE, THE OTHER SIDE OF THE STORY
    - BY MICHAEL PASSAGLIA ...................................... 75

**ABOUT THE AUTHOR**

    ANGELIQUEA PASSAGLIA ....................................... 85

**RESOURCES** ................................................................... 91

# INTRODUCTION

I have always found women fascinating, complex, and intriguing. I have even been accused of staring. I swear I'm not! I simply love people watching (okay maybe I am staring a little).

We come in all sizes, shapes, colors and styles. Some of us are happy-go-lucky, others are very serious; some are quite exquisite, while others are adventurous and athletic. The list of differences goes on and on, which is why y'all fascinate me.

We do have a few things in common though regardless of who we as women have consciously or unconsciously become. We all have vaginas, periods, hormones, and quite frankly, we all go through menopause. Yes, we all have and love our boobies too, but for this book, they don't make the cut.

I am a storyteller, and in this book, I am going to tell you many captivating stories about menopause to show you how to get through it, where to seek guidance, and how to laugh about this journey. At the very least, you'll laugh at me and my journey as well as some of my girlfriends' stories.

I am not going to hold back. This book is for the lady who wants to get down and dirty about menopause, find guidance to help her get through this kick-ass time, and hopefully come out the other side intact—not looking like she just walked out of the scene in *Mr. and Mrs. Smith* when the house blew up! (Although I bet Mrs. Smith's menopause is more glamorous than mine . . . .)

Please! This book is not medical advice. I strongly encourage you to seek out professionals and advocate for yourself. I especially encourage those of you who have or had cancer to ask your chosen cancer specialist about any alternative menopause therapies.

# CHAPTER 1

## WHERE DID MY PERIOD GO?

That is a great question (and one you may be asking yourself now), but the full story actually started a few years prior to my period's disappearance.

Let me set the stage for you... I was out drinking wine, listening to a friend of mine gossip about one of her other friends. I actually love hearing stories this way; I get all the fun drama and details, then head back to my drama-free life giggling a bit. Did I just write drama-free life? Well, that's untrue! I definitely have drama, ladies, just nowhere near as much as the old me. Isn't that funny in retrospect, the decades before perimenopause and menopause

I had copious amounts of drama. Now my main drama is menopause!

Back to my story . . . my friend was explaining to me that her girlfriend was wearing white pants and had a blood bomb at work. Anything called a blood bomb must be bad, and this gal works with all men—even worse! My immediate thought was, girl, get your shit together! We have all been having periods since we were about thirteen—you should be prepared. Plus, who at this point in life doesn't know old Aunt Rose is showing up? My friend then tells me that she has been having periods so bad that she can't even use tampons. Okay, that's weird! I think she must have cancer or something.

Fast-forward to several months after that meeting with my bud for wine. It's my nephew's graduation, and I'm attending with my parents and my stepson. There I am sitting between my dad and my stepson wearing the cutest blue and white striped shorts and—*Wait, what?!* What is *that*? It can't be my period, that ended a few days ago. Oh my God, whatever it is, it's running down my leg. *Ohhhhh!* This is a blood bomb! I quickly wrap my sweater around me, say a quick hello to my nephew, and run out of the football stadium. Holy crap! What is going on with me?! Of course, I immediately type a description of that situation into my search engine when I arrive home. All signs point to *menopause*. No, it can't be. I am only forty-five. Something is wrong!

The next day I get in touch with my OB-GYN. When I finally get in to see her, she breaks the news that I am premenopausal based on my recent experience and lab work. What is *that*? How do I fix it? Her response is, "You don't. Ask your mom how hers went." That's it?! That's her medical advice? I begrudgingly accept it, and while walking out of her office I phone my mom. She says, "Sorry honey, I had a hysterectomy at thirty-five," as did her mother and her sister. I call my girlfriends who are older than me; they all share that they did something called an ablation, which basically fries and scars your insides so no egg can attach, and no period can happen.

I contact my OB-GYN again to schedule an ablation. By the time I finally get in to see her, my life has gotten steadily worse. The blood bombs occur monthly and are part of the heaviest periods I have *ever* had. It's so bad I can't even leave my house when I am having a period. I plead with my doctor that it feels as though my uterus is actually falling out, and I may die if she doesn't perform this procedure. She assures me she's onboard, no problem. I just need to have a few more appointments first and get my health insurance company's approval. With this country's kick-ass, super-efficient healthcare system, a few appointments and a health insurance approval take some time.

*Three months later* I finally get the call to schedule my much-awaited procedure. Yay! I am over-the-moon excited. I am counting down how many more periods I will have. Finally, this pain and embarrassment will all come to an end. This entire process has taken about four months. Because it took so long, we are now in a new calendar year and my insurance carrier is now requiring its $3K deductible before my procedure. Ugh! Okay. Fine! I am not happy, but I am desperate and will do whatever it takes.

During this same time my sister-in-law, who is also my best friend and confident, passes away. I decide to travel and be with my family out of state for a month to just be there and offer any help I can. I also want to be around people and things that remind me of her. This means I have to reschedule my procedure. What I didn't know then was that the extra three months I was going to have to wait for a new procedure date was actually a true blessing. It gave me time to slow down and decide if this was truly the right path for me.

In my research I heard so many conflicting pros and cons of the ablation procedure. Then I started to reflect on the fact that messing with God's work has never really worked out fabulously for me (we can chat about that later)! I began talking with lots of women. It was seriously disturbing to do this! Everyone had a horror story one way or another. What was even worse is that I found nothing published to read, and my doctor's advice was to ask my mom?! Trust me, this is why I've written *Here Comes Menopause!*—so you don't have to go through the confusion and frustrations I did.

Ultimately, I made the decision to let nature take its course. I felt like this was the best decision ever! As months went by the blood bombs subsided, and my period seemed to become regular again. Just about the time I decided I was no longer premenopausal . . . no period. This was fantastic!

The first month your period doesn't show up, you sort of forget how awful you felt before. You feel fantastic: no period, no PMS, none of the painful symptoms of perimenopause. You might have one small moment of: OMG—what if I am pregnant?! Then you realize you are in menopause.

Day by day you get this insecure feeling. Should I be packing around tampons? Just about the time you accept the fact that your period is truly over, you get PMS. It doesn't make sense at all! So, this is how this goes . . . you have PMS for a little over a week with no period. Everything is swollen, you're wishing and praying your period would just start so you can finally feel better. Except it doesn't. You just get to hang out and suffer. Then one day you wake up feeling fantastic, the swelling goes away, and tada! You are back on track for no period and feeling fantastic.

Month three rolls around with no period . . . then suddenly you get your period. No warning, no PMS, nothing! Just a heavy crappy period. Again, you may feel insecure about what your body is putting you through. It's like April rain in California. It comes in hot and then it's done a few days later. My doctor told me that once I go twelve months without a period, I am done having periods forever.

Well, I was good to go for three months, then I started the twelve-month clock over again—and over and over again. This cycle lasted several years for me. It did seem like the times I hung out with younger women, particularly my niece, who is well below the perimenopause timeframe, I then had a period . . . no science here ladies. This was just my observation. We can call it my hormone conspiracy theory.

This process of going from perimenopause to full-blown menopause is a long journey. It's a marathon. I honestly believed early on that this wasn't going to happen to me . . . I crack myself up.

It is safe to say the terrain is not always the same. You do not feel miserable all the time, and you are not always on your heaviest period ever. Your bad days will be bad, expect that. The rest of the time you will have so many other fun things to focus on, like hot flashes, brain fog, weight gain, and more.

# CHAPTER 2

# WOW! I AM SO HOT!

Hot flashes are why I am so HOT! When trying to understand why I have them, I heard straight from the doctor's mouth, "We don't know what causes them." I am here to tell the genius it's got to be a decrease and fluctuation in our estrogen . . . maybe research that, Dr. Smarty Pants. Just one aging lady's guess.

I am going to break this down into four types of hot flashes. I have a nickname for each type I had and a detailed description. Enjoy! Perhaps you've experienced some of these. If I am missing a type you've had, please let me know; I'm happy to add it to the list. Also, I'll be glad it was one I didn't experience.

The four types of hot flashes I experienced are:

1. Heat surge
2. Sweaty flash
3. Night drench
4. Generally hot

I will start with the heat surge because that's the first hot flash my body experienced. These surges began around the time my period started to go haywire. There was no warning whatsoever. I was sitting there just feeling warm around the back of my neck. If you feel this, you will absolutely think something is up. Then you start to feel a prickly feeling all over your body. You're not too hot, but you do feel warmer than usual. What confused me was the dizzy feeling. Then as soon as it comes on, it goes away. Please do not think you are such a kick-ass chick that this is the end of your hot flashes. That is your mind lying to you. The rest of the hot flash types will show up, just give them time.

After that first hot flash, some time passes and then a new flavor of flash shows up. I call this the sweaty flash. This was my number one most unfavorable flash. Like all of them, I received zero notice. When you feel this flash, you will suddenly be sweating profusely. Sweat comes dripping down your face, and your hair looks like it did when you danced for hours in a club at twenty-one years old. Your bra is filled with sweat. When it keeps coming back, you will learn pack an additional pair of panties, bra, shirt and towel wherever you go. I almost forgot to mention, you'll want to have a hair clip on hand too. You're welcome. Makeup is funny. It simply melts right off.

This sweaty flash is the devil. It doesn't care if you are in a business meeting, dolled up for a night out, or in the middle of trying to get yourself ready to head out of the house. It is so bizarre to people watching you experience it that you just have to say you're having a hot flash. I found it to be quite embarrassing. My husband thought it was hilarious and seemed to think outing my menopause was some type of badge of honor I had just received. When this type of flash decided to morph into a new type I couldn't have been happier. The rest of them are truly easy compared to this one.

The next type of flash I named night drench. Night sweats my ass! This flash type is the second worst. After I suffered through my sweaty flash phase I went several months with no hot flashes. I thought I was a rockstar, and the good Lord had decided I was such a good human that I deserved to complete my menopause hot flash free. One night I woke up completely drenched: my nighty, pillow, sheets, everything. I was so wet I needed a towel to dry off. This isn't the usual night sweat you get when you are ill. You are in a pool of water. Here is the fun part—once you're done sweating, then you are freezing cold.

This nightly cycle can run several hours or all night long. Hot, freezing, repeat. You only sleep a few hours at a time, then awake again to dry off, change, grab new bedding, and freeze, then fall asleep. You are exhausted. This type of hot flash can really wear you down.

With the final type of hot flash, generally hot, I wish we were speaking of my appearance. This is the phase I am still in, and I have a feeling this one lasts a while. The upside is that this is the easiest of them all and very tolerable. On occasion you will feel mildly warm. It's barely noticeable after everything you have already been through. I do fear I will be in this phase for decades though. As I sit here typing away, my glasses fog up from another one of these hot flashes. It just is what it is. You can get through it; *we* can get through it! We can do hard things! We are women!

I did accidentally discover a temporary relief for these hot flashes. Trust me, I tried all the over-the-counter hot flash relief—save your money! They did nothing. Annually, my girlfriends and I take a girls' wine trip. We usually rent a house and bring all the food and supplies for an amazing weekend. One of us bought THC gummies to enhance our at-home facial experience. As we laughed and laughed, we had no idea what we would discover two days later. *Side note*: THC gummies are legal where we live.

I finally slept after taking those gummies, and so did my girlfriend who was going through the same hot flashes. Two nights later I said to my friend Tamera, "Have you had hot flashes since we have been here?" She looked shocked and said, "No". "Do you think it's the weed?" I asked. She started laughing and said, "Oh my gawd, yes!" It was so amazing to finally have relief.

I started using the THC gummies at a dose and frequency of half of five milligrams once a week. Then I took that dose every ten days, then every two weeks until my hot flashes were very few and much more tolerable. I have heard rumor the CBD also has this effect. I did not try CBD gummies, so I can't comment on them. In the end, I didn't want to be on THC. For me, it was fun once a year, out in the middle of nowhere with a couple girlfriends, but needing it continuously was an internal problem for me. So, this journey with me and the gummies ended, as did the relief from the hot flashes.

Hot flash medication seems to be in my social media feed constantly. I have not indulged in any, but I have done some research. In spring of 2023 the FDA approved a drug that may reduce the frequency or the severity of hot flashes. You see, when our estrogen is falling off the cliff, our brain is confused about exactly how to regulate our temperature. This new drug is supposed to help that struggling brain function better. It's not a hormone. So, for those of us who are choosing a non-hormone route, this could be the answer. I did my research at Harvard Health Publishing Medical School. If you want a more robust explanation, I recommend checking out what they have to say.

Hormone replacement therapy (HRT) is my huckleberry. For me, it covers several of the problems I am dealing with due to menopause. Each issue is very important all by itself, so to do HRT, which annihilates the hot flashes in just a few days was a no-brainer. I do a deep dive into HRT in Chapter 4.

One upside to hot flashes is that they could increase the laughter between you and your partner. One day I was standing in my kitchen, greeting my husband after work, and I started to unbutton my blouse. He looked at me like the heavens opened up, and I greeted him with a big, "Yes!" Then I added, "I'm having a hot flash, Hun, not trying to turn you on." As we both started laughing together, I realized that moment summed up our relationship right now.

> "It's never too late to be what you might have been."
> — George Eliot

# CHAPTER 3

# WEIGHT GAIN

Naturally, I was hoping I would lose weight from all that I sweated out during the hot flashes. It only makes sense, right?

Again, here I am with my doctor. "So, I have gained ten to thirteen pounds," I say. She says, "Yes, I noticed that. You're definitely going to gain weight, maybe even up to twenty pounds. People like you that have never had belly fat will struggle with this." Inside my head I'm thinking, What the f*ck?! She then says, "I recommend a plant-based diet, and overall, you don't need as many calories as you used to." Again, my inside voice screams, What the f*ck?!

I would like to say I have no words for the solid medical advice given. However, as we all know by now, I am a tad mouthy . . . I can't even hear what else she is telling me about the stupid colonoscopy and boob squeeze, a.k.a. mammogram, she is referring me to. Inside my head the crazy redhead in me is having a full-on bitch fit, which is basically what I have been doing for five plus years.

But let's get back to my weight. This is a lifelong subject for most of us ladies. I have always been active and naturally on the lighter side. This doesn't mean I haven't struggled my entire life with my weight and body image. For God's sake, we grew up with the Victoria Secret models and MTV videos; we have *very* unrealistic body images.

My journey started around age thirteen, and it's safe to say I am still riding that bronco. With effort I have always been able to control my weight if it swayed in the direction I didn't want it to go. To gain weight when I eat healthy, workout all the time, and do my best at not drinking all the wine in Napa is a real kick in the gut. It feels hopeless.

We are in a world of information, suggestions, and advice. The diets out there are endless, and some are quite confusing. Every time I get on social media I see a new diet, theory, or pill. How the hell can we be in the information era and still not know what to do? It is too much information, and I think it is designed to confuse us.

I have been on enough diets to know if it's not something you can stick to *for life*, then don't waste your time and your money. Once you return to your old habits, all of the pounds will just creep right back on. It's devastating. So now walking onto this battlefield of menopause we know the weight is coming. Be kind to yourself and give yourself some grace.

I don't think we need to research much to figure out our food is jacked up here in America. I am always amazed after traveling to Europe and eating pasta and bread daily that I am lighter than when I left. I have had friends tell me it's because I am walking everywhere. Bullshit! I never workout on vacation, and like many of us, either my phone or watch tells me my calories burned for the day. It is the same when I travel as it is at home when I include my workout. Our food in America is different!

We have fast food restaurants everywhere, and that food is chock-full of trans fats and sugar. Many of us are part of a two-income family and as a result, we seldom have the luxury of a big, healthy sit-down dinner these days. Even when we eat at a restaurant and try to order a healthy meal, we can't guarantee exactly what we are getting.

I am not a dietician or a nutritionist, but I know you really can't go wrong eating lean protein and fresh, organic fruits, vegetables, and nuts. Read the ingredients of everything you buy! Or better yet, buy whole, organically grown foods with no list of ingredients instead of packaged foods. Look, I too wasn't happy about the extra prices to buy organic. However, let me share why I am all-in on that nowadays.

I live near orchards and see the workers in the orchards wearing hazmat suits with face ventilators while spraying our food. You simply can't convince me that I am not ingesting those chemicals when I eat that food. In fact, I no longer take my dogs into the orchards because twice now my dogs have been poisoned by arsenic while on our morning walk through the orchards.

Stay away from sugar; this is a big one. Pick up the book *Sugar Blues* by William Dufty. You're in for a surprise. This book was written in 1975, and you will absolutely be in shock reading it, especially because it was written over fifty years ago. It might even piss you off! A client of mine gave it to me to read in my twenties, and that was the end of my sugar addiction. It's absolutely a real thing.

Lift weights often; heavy weights seem to be my secret sauce. Try to lift three times a week for thirty to forty minutes, and get mild cardio in on the regular. To be clear, I don't recommend hurt-your-back heavy weightlifting; "heavy" to me means lifting more than fifteen pounds. If you have an injury and are unable to lift that much or more, just do what you can. Something is better than nothing. You will *not* turn into a giant muscle builder by lifting heavier weights. I promise you. Muscle takes up half the space of body fat. People assigned female at birth cannot get the results to look like Arnold

Schwarzenegger without utilizing body-enhancing drugs.

As far as cardio workouts go, get a walk in a few times a week. If you feel like you can do more, then do it. Right now, people are loving pickleball, and that counts! This is about so much more than tapering off the weight. It's about mobility, warding off osteoporosis, controlling your blood pressure, and more. Be sure to stretch too, and make it a part of your exercise routine so you don't feel like you have a giant to-do list for staying healthy.

Another hot topic right now is fascia stretching. This involves working with your connective tissues to make them more elastic and durable. Fascia stretching can release muscle tension, increase mobility, and improve overall body composition and flexibility. The practice of fascia stretching is taking over the massage therapy space. Truth be told, I go a few times a month, even more if I can. It truly beats the hell out of getting a massage in terms of benefits, and now I think of massage more as relaxation. If you can find a massage therapist who incorporates fascia stretching, you are winning!

Do your best with these healthy practices. Knowing weight gain is likely to happen during menopause, invest in stretchy jeans and shirts with wide bottoms. You will still be a cutie with a couple extra pounds on. As far as the plant-based diet goes, wine is from a plant . . . just kidding . . . kind of.

Since I have started this book, another medication came on the market. *The shot.* You know the one. Just like that, with almost no medical supervision, you can order the weight loss shot, give it to yourself, and lose weight. When it came out on the market, I was curious and also jealous of my friends who were dropping ten, twenty, even thirty pounds without much effort. What I noticed is that they ate very little. I have heard concerns about massive muscle loss while on the shot. Again, I do not think it's a be-all, end-all solution. If you decide to go forward with the shot, make sure you eat a high protein diet and figure out how you're going to control your appetite once you stop the shot. It's pretty expensive, so you don't want to go through this cost, achieve weight loss, and then gain it all back. If you choose to take the shot, I'd love to hear your feedback and story of your experience.

One last thought on this topic is to stop trying to be your weight and physique you were at twenty. You're not twenty anymore, you have curves, and you are a woman. Go own it, because you are absolutely beautiful and amazing.

# CHAPTER 4

# LET'S TALK ABOUT SEX

I promised my husband I would not share our sex life with all of you. All of the fun, sexy, impromptu, spontaneous sex is off limits . . . but, if I am being fully honest, I have to share *some* things to come full circle and offer a greater understanding of how sex changes during menopause. This chapter will have oodles of goodies and experiences including perspectives from men who love us and are dealing with our changing bodies the best way they can.

One evening I'm sitting at a bar with my friend wasting time while on a conference work trip. A bar is a bar. People want to chat with us and the "what you do" and "where you are from" questions come up. Since we are there for a conference, lots of the patrons in the bar are in similar careers. My friend busts out with the opener, "She is writing a book about menopause." In a bar full of men, this was heckled at first. Quite honestly, I wouldn't be writing a book about it if I wasn't one hundred percent able to get into the conversation without blushing. I am what I am, and I am in menopause.

A gentleman sitting to my left leans in and starts in on a twenty-minute diatribe about his wife going through menopause and how it's affecting their marriage. To say his words were insightful is an understatement. In my own personal life, with my ever-so-patient husband, I have seen, felt, and worked on overcoming the beating my marriage has taken while I navigate menopause.

I am truly blessed to have a husband so willing to discuss the challenges from his point of view *and* hear me out in trying to understand my new body, inside and out. Oftentimes when you walk through the valley of hell you forget to look around and see how your actions or inaction have affected other people, especially your life partner. Did I just call menopause the valley of hell? It's okay, I am good with that, it's accurate.

This conversation morphed into an entire bar talking about this subject, and over the following days of the conference I had multiple people walk up to me to talk about menopause. I somehow turned into the person who has the answers. Both men and women had questions for me. Men mostly had questions about sex or lack of it, as well as questions about reconnecting with their wife. Women wanted to know how to control weight gain, handle hot flashes, and make choices about HRT.

That night at the bar, the gentleman sitting next to me seemed so heartbroken about the fact that when he tries to touch his wife she pulls away. Or when he tries to get intimate with her it falls on deaf ears. He feels like he is no longer wanted by her, and the things she has tried for relief of menopause symptoms either made her gain weight or failed to work. He shared with me he's deeply in love and completely at a loss.

This brings me to my husband. He shared a similar conversation with me about us. During that initial conversation I was thinking to myself, "Seriously?! I'm going through all of this, and now you are telling me you're frustrated our sex life has changed? Ugh!" He was right though. Everything had changed, and I had no idea. I was just trying to not sweat to death, recall what I'm doing today, not gain weight, not be moody, not snap at someone, and try to figure out what the hell I did with my glasses. I truly had no idea how I didn't think about having sex. I just didn't.

I wasn't feeling horny. Sure, I was aroused the times we were having sex, but I wasn't actively thinking about it during the day. I wasn't planning a romantic encounter with my husband. I wasn't buying sexy lingerie or even flirting with my husband, as we always had throughout the day, throughout the years. I made up excuses to myself and to him: we've been together forever, we are in a different season of our marriage, etc. I went as far as telling him a story about an old friend who is recently married, and her new husband isn't understanding why they are not having sex. Menopause! Then telling him, and believing it, I said, "Thank God that's not us."

I believed everything was normal between us. I thought the issue was his; I felt completely like myself in that area. We talked about it not being normal, and I kept promising him that things were getting better, and I started pretending they were. I made an effort to actually schedule in our sex, so as not to forgot to have sex later in the day. Of course I didn't share this with him, I just did it. As months went by, he and I both started feeling the disconnect in our relationship. He said to me one day, "This feels forced, or like it is on your chore list." Oh my God, he knows, I thought. Now I have to deal with this. I had to explain something to him I didn't understand myself.

I started to think about all the women I know who went through a divorce at this time. I remember a lady on the treadmill next to me at the gym telling me a story about her friend who went "crazy" during menopause and ended up leaving her husband. I recall other stories of men leaving their wives for a younger version. Yeah, I get it . . . you mean one who's not in menopause? Kinda makes sense. It was like the light turned on for me. This was messing up my marriage.

Once the truth was out, it was out. I went back to the doctor. It sure would be nice if they just handed me a list of shit that goes wrong during menopause. That would be helpful. My OB-GYN talked to me about hormone replacement therapy, HRT. We did my labs, and she said, well, you are in perimenopause, and you can definitely do HRT. She was all for progesterone and/or estrogen. I needed to do the research, so I did neither right then.

I remember my mom being on Premarin, and I recalled she didn't care for it. During the same timeframe I walked into the office I go to for my Medi Spa services, and there is a big sign that says: Superior Hormone Pellet Therapy. The list of symptoms to qualify for it was low libido, brain fog, mood swings, weight gain, and lack of motivation. Yes, yes, yes, yes, and yes. I couldn't believe it. Here I am for my skin, and I think I found my people for menopause treatments. My mind was racing. This doctor is amazing. She is a few years younger than I am and has practiced medicine for over twenty years, then shifted her career into building a Medi Spa. She found her passion, took all the courses, and went for it. I actually did find my people.

The Medi Spa owner and I discussed my skin and HRT therapy for about an hour. Something stuck with me about the information she shared on HRT. She said the pellets are bioidentical. Did you read that? *Bio-identical,* so they are natural, plant-based substances that metabolize in our bodies. These pellets are testosterone, estrogen, or both.

She gave me a lab slip, I wasted no time, and drove right to the lab. I felt like the lady in *My Cousin Vinny* when she is stomping on the front porch freaking out about her biological clock ticking. No patience whatsoever! Unfortunately, you have to wait five to eight days to get the results of the lab test. I am a wreck! Please, for the love of God, fix me!

After about a week I was summoned to my doctor's office to get my results. I turns out I am low on testosterone. Oh geez. My husband is going to razz me about Low T . . . but, whatever . . . give me the pellets, and give them to me now! I have no idea why I had to come back for the pellet insertion appointment another time. It was probably some kind of karma for being impatient at another time in my life.

A week later, it is finally the day. Laying there with my butt cheek in the air, quick numbing and a pinch and voila. I am with pellets! I am very excited and head back to my daily life. Several hours later my husband comes home from work. As we sat debriefing one another regarding our day he says, "What's different?" I am over the moon with excitement. He noticed something was different. I felt like Mel Gibson yelling FREEDOM!!!! I went nuts talking to my husband about my pellets. I remember saying to him, "What do you see that's different? I mean I know I am a tad chatty, but what else other than that?" It was my whole being. I hadn't even noticed how lifeless and unhappy I had been feeling. I wasn't depressed, but I certainly wasn't happy. That was my first noticeable indication that something had significantly improved.

As the days went by after my first pellet insertion, my mood improved, my brain fog diminished, I had increased motivation to complete tasks, and I just felt happy. A few weeks into this treatment, suddenly I felt a tingling down there. Weird, I had forgotten that that happens. Can it be?

Did I just get my libido back? It is not the libido of my twenties, but we are back in action!

Now I must address the weight. I gained about three pounds from the hormones. I was told that may happen and that it's water weight. It took a few months for that weight to come off. Overall, I found it was easier to look leaner.

If HRT is the path you choose, give it time to work in your body. Don't give up after three months and jump ship. They're hormones that we need to get used to, body and mind. Take your time to research the options out there. We are all made differently. What worked for me, may not be the best fit for you.

In talking to my husband, he is and was in alignment with the path I took. He also shared with me that he deeply missed the old me and shared that it just wasn't as much fun being my husband, but he knew it was still great, and he had signed up for better or worse. I share that with you so you know how menopause is truly affecting everyone around you. Talk to your life partner about what you are going through, try to have fun with it, and have each other's back.

If you discover one HRT is no longer working for you or you feel like the one you chose isn't for you, don't give up; try another type. I was on just the testosterone pellets for one year. I would say the first six months were the best. Certainly, I felt way better with them than I felt without them.

Then I started to noticed peaks and valleys in libido, weight fluctuation, light mood swings, and the occasional hot flash again. After another trip to the lab, we discovered it was time to add estrogen and progestogen to the pellet mix. I am still sticking with the pellets for now. I am not a doctor, and this is just a story about what works for me.

I have friends who are on hormone creams as well as estrogen pills. I even have some friends who are just going to deal with the menopause journey with no outside help. One also happens to be my friend who's not going to fight going gray . . . I love her, but I can't be her. I have found the help I need through HRT, and I hope you find what you need in the way that's best for you.

# CHAPTER 5

# TO BOTOX OR NOT TO BOTOX?

I try to get a little cardio in with a girlfriend on a regular basis. My neighbor and friend, Cheri, and I would knock out a few miles of running or walking three or more days a week. As we were chatting away, she says to me one day, "Ang, what's wrong with your forehead?" Well, I have no idea what she is taking about! What's wrong with it? She explains to me that the upper portion of my forehead is moving while I am talking, and the lower part is not. Oh no! What have I done?! I did Botox several days earlier . . . could that be the problem? It turns out to be the exact problem.

## Botox

I went in to see my dermatologist because I am fair-skinned, with blue eyes and auburn hair. According to the powers that be, that combo is the secret sauce for skin cancer. I have the awesome pleasure of standing naked in front of some stranger while he examines every inch of my body annually. Not fun! *Side note*: make sure your dermatologist is not attractive.

After my dermatologist gives me the thumbs-up on my skin, he tells me he can fix that little crease between my eyes with Botox. That sounds great to me, and I'm in! So, after I leave the office, I immediately check my rearview mirror for my new look. Nothing! It's the same. I go home and get a good night's rest. Then I wake up to go check out my new Hollywood Botox brow. Nothing! Literally nothing has changed. How can this be? Then a few days later I am suddenly unable to make facial movements I used to. It's working! My spot in between my eyes is frozen! Fantastic! Well, it was fantastic until I was told that the upper portion of my forehead moves, but the lower portion does not.

The thing with Botox is it takes three to four months to go away. After a few months of hazing from my friend and husband, it's time for another appointment. I have decided to get the entire forehead frozen. This will fix the situation once and for all.

It was perfect. I am so freaking youthful now! So here is the thing about Botox: it paralyzes your facial muscles by making them fatigue and get weak. I originally thought this was great. The weaker the muscle, the less I will have to get this poison pumped into my forehead.

This is the era of selfies, or us-ies, as my hubby and I call them. We were snapping pictures and sending them to our family when I noticed this thing on the side of my nose. It's a giant muscle in my face. Could it have gotten stronger while the upper portion of my face was getting weaker because I had not poisoned it? I believe it did! Awesome! Remember how I wrote earlier that messing with God's work never worked out fabulously for me? This was a perfect case in point! What was I doing to myself? I was making things worse.

I started really taking a close look at my parents. My mom always used luxurious creams on her face, got regular facials, and tended to her skin like it was The Queen's Diamond. She looks ten to fifteen years younger than her actual age. Then I took a look at my papa. He has never even used face cream, let alone tended to any of his skin. He also looks ten to fifteen years younger than his actual age. Could it just be genetics? It definitely plays a giant role in how your skin will fair during the aging process.

My experience now gives me the right to advise you before you start a Botox treatment. Check out your elderly family member's skin. This should be the beginning point of your skin care regime, especially during menopause.

## Facial Creams

Now that I have been Botox-free and allowing another part of my body to also let nature take its course, the facial cream cocktail begins. I use a heavy facial cream, retinol, and vitamin C serum. Do not forget sunscreen—I have to write that in, or my dermatologist might cancel culture me. The other obvious takeaways for skincare are: stay out of the sun, hydrate, eat well, and get enough sleep. I am not talking dramatic results here but simply sustaining what I already have.

Instead of Botox, let's dive into facials, lasers, and microneedling. I found myself very confused by all the options. I took this journey with baby steps. My entire mantra was: do everything to avoid the facelift. So, it begins. Facials: get facials, and get them often. Schedule yourself a lovely hydrating facial at least once a month. I like to mix it into the day I get my hair done; I love the added pampering time. Plus, my hair/facial lady is one of my good friends, so it's just plain fun and laughs.

## Facials

Pick yourself up all the hydration facial masks at your local drug store. Use them weekly. Yes, you do look like Jason from Friday the 13th. Lie back in your favorite spot in the house or backyard and enjoy the peace and quiet while you moisturize your beautiful face.

Or, my personal favorite, have your besties over, pour Champagne, and enjoy one another. The fact that you all look like Jason just adds to the laughter. Unless you are like my friend Tina—she somehow even looks amazing looking like Jason. She is definitely a unicorn.

I do want to share my experience with the photo facial, or intense pulsed light (IPL) therapy. This one felt almost like electric pulses. I was jumpy. The photo facial decreases the appearance of dark spots. Excess melanin production, which can result from aging or sun exposure, is what causes these annoying dark spots.

These spots are benign and typically don't need to be treated; their appearance can be lessened or eliminated for aesthetic purposes. Treatment alternatives can be provided by a dermatologist as well as over the counter lightening creams.

Let's go back to avoiding the sun and wearing sunscreen on a daily basis. This can help prevent dark spots. Seriously, do not go outside without mineral sunscreen on your face, neck, and hands. Period! Once those dark spots come out, it's their job to keep coming out. So, you need to get on them and keep on them. I have a few spots, and this is why I included the photo facial in my anti-aging process. I have freckles, have always had them, and they have been drastically reduced after this facial. I'm not mad about that.

## Lasers

Lasers are... Laser resurfacing uses a device to remove the appearance of wrinkles and scars in the skin. It can also even out skin coloring and tighten skin. My experience with lasers is...

I was contemplating a chemical peel when I discovered the option of microneedling. I worried about the chemical peel because I tend to get keloid scarring. I talked to my dermatologist about it, and that doctor had the same concern about my scar history. One of my friends told me she had much better results with microneedling than she did with her chemical peels. Well, that settled it—microneedling it is.

I did three treatments over the course of two months. There was no down time, little pain, and easy after care. I was surprised that the results came over the course of six months. Fine lines slowly disappeared and deep lines are not as pronounced. I truly love my results and will definitely keep this up once a year moving forward.

What about the neck? Our necks need attention! We have a laser for that too! Start early before your skin gets frumpy and sags. Like anything, the sooner you get to it, the better off you'll be. My first neck treatment was a tad scary. I did it after I did microneedling and photo facial. I was expecting the type of pain those gave me. I kept thinking my neck doesn't have any fat to shoulder the pain. Fun fact, it's painless! It feels as gentle as an ultrasound with gel for your stomach. Most of us have had that done. The wand gets warm, and just about the time you feel like you have had enough it is over.

The neck laser resurfacing I did involved a series of five sessions, once a week. I left the office with a tinge of redness that went away after a few hours. I really started to notice the skin tighten up after about the third session. This is not a neck lift, so don't think you are going to get those types of results. I did have several people ask me if I had lost weight. That, my friends, is the result!

## Skincare Must-Haves

I just want to note quickly some skin care routine must-haves during menopause. We know we need gentle facial cleaner, a good moisturizer, vitamin C, Tretinoin Cream, and Hyaluronic Serum. Some people are on the fence about an eye cream, some love it, some are all good without it. Because that skin is very delicate, be sure to choose wisely.

Taking care of your skin is just like taking care of the rest of you. The good news is since you are already doing all the good things for your body, your skin will thank you.

## Sculptra

There is a new injectable on the market that is actually quite amazing called Sculptra. It helps with the collagen rebuilding that we so desperately need to keep looking our youthful selves, if that's our goal. According to Sculptra, "The skin needs collagen to resist signs of aging, such as fine lines, wrinkles, and sagging. By age forty, most of us have lost up to 30 percent of our collagen within five years of menopause. Sculptra helps stimulate natural collagen production.[6] The poly-L-lactic acid in Sculptra forms a framework that helps support and maintain the skin's inner structure, which may lead to a more youthful-looking appearance." Sculptra is injected into your face, in the areas that you and your doctor see fit. You have three different sessions, and then you're good to go with this youthful face for the next two years.

Honestly, as much as this aging gig sucks, we are aging at the best time. There are so many amazing products and procedures out there these days, and I only see it getting better. Dare I say Stem Cells . . . .

## Stem Cells

One example I've found of stem cell usage for facial rejuvenation is Platelet Rich Plasma Face Lift. PRP Face Lift is a procedure developed for people who want healthy, youthful, and rejuvenating skin. This procedure is a rather quick process that does not require surgery. The PRP Face Lift procedure involves using Juvéderm to restore shape following by injecting PRP below the dermis to help restore color and texture along with enhancing a normal shape. This non-surgical facelift is a skin treatment that uses the body's own natural healing and growth factors that are derived from your blood."

## Red Light Therapy

Red light therapy is yet another form of skin treatment that can keep our skin in ideal shape. With red light therapy you expose your skin to a lamp, device, or laser with a red light. It uses an LED that emits the correct spectrum of light. When the light enters your skin, your mitochondria soak it up and make more energy, which helps cells repair themselves. Red light therapy uses very low levels of heat and doesn't hurt or burn the skin. Does it work? Research is ongoing. More research needs to be done, there is some evidence that it may be useful for several health and beauty concerns.

## Hair Growth

As you go through menopause, you may be asking yourself, Are my eyebrows getting thinner? Am I losing my hair?

They sure are and you sure are, unless you are Brook Shields or Christy Brinkley. You can blame hair loss on lots of things: thyroid, bad eating habits, lack of proper supplements, working out too much, too much alcohol, DNA, stress, and the biggie—hormones. So back when y'all were birthing babies and recovering from childbirth, remember your hair loss? Well friends, the same thing happens during menopause.

Your hormones are on a ten-to-fifteen-year rollercoaster, and for some of us, this wreaks havoc on our hair. Vitamin D3 and Biotin are supposed to help. I do take these, but I cannot tell you that they've helped. I also use a home remedy of cinnamon and rosemary that I spray on my hair and scalp. My hair seems to be slightly growing back and growing faster than it has in a very long time. Many of us are on recovery from COVID hair loss. You may find yourself asking, is this COVID or is this menopause? Ugh . . . it can be hard to tell.

Minoxidil is another tried and true remedy for some for hair growth. I did try it, and I truly saw no noticeable results, but that could just be me. Now my girlfriend takes oral Minoxidil, and not only does she swear by it, but I can see a huge difference. She takes half a pill daily, and her doctor told her if she took one pill a day, she would see better results, but she would also get some facial hair. These are the things we deal with now . . . full head of hair *and* a freaking beard as well?! I do know that you must continue to take the pill.

At the time I was contemplating taking it myself I thought, I don't want to take medication if I don't have to. Now I am thinking, full head of hair and all I have to do is take a tiny pill daily. And maybe get laser hair removal on my face—ha!

Alma TED™ is another advancement in hair restoration procedures. "It is an ultrasound-based system that comes with a patented Tip technology engineered with Impact Delivery™. This device works on a unique pushback effect via air pressure developed to complement your hair restoration treatment outcomes when used with topical products." I have personally witnessed a close male friend doing this hair restoration. It works. It's not cheap, and you do have to keep it up, but it definitely works.

One other solution is a procedure called Platelet Rich Plasma (PRP). I am super interested in this, but I haven't tried it. This is the exact procedure for The PRP facelift mentioned earlier. The doctor takes a couple vials of blood and separates the plasma from the blood. Then the plasma is injected into the scalp to promote hair growth. You do three or four of these treatments.

It turns out this procedure is pretty amazing for lots of different areas of the body. They draw your own blood and immediately spin your blood to separate the Platelet Rich Plasma from the red blood cells and inject the plasma back into you. This procedure was originally thought to help rejuvenate cartilage in the knee. Now they have discovered ways to stimulate wound healing, as well as grow skin, cartilage, bone, and hair. Later we will discuss how this procedure improves your sex. It's so exciting!

> "You are never too old to set another goal or to dream a new dream." – C.S. Lewis

# CHAPTER 6

# OUR VAGINA

Isn't she lovely? Isn't she wonderful? Isn't she precious? I don't think Stevie Wonder was discussing the vagina, but I am!

We have things to discuss here . . . where do I start? Incontinence? Orgasm abilities? Rejuvenation? Vaginal dryness? Let's discuss them all.

## Incontinence

This is the absolute worst. Here I thought because I had not given birth my superstar vagina was just going to slide right past this one . . . nope! I was on a long walk with my workout girlfriend chatting and sweating, and I was almost home. I was only one hundred yards from my bathroom. I can hold it! Nope, turns out I can't. Is 'dollop' the right description? It wasn't much, but it was more than not at all, and I was mortified. Great news, now I am peeing my pants. What's next, adult diapers?

I do have a friend who has no shame in her game and sports adult diapers. I am just not going down that path now. I searched online for Kegel exercises and bought those small, metal Ben Wa balls (weird). I have found the balls are no big deal to hold in there. But the thought of those little guys just chilling up there makes me have to go with a no.

The Kegel exercises are okay, but along with everything else I do daily, it definitely slips off the to-do list quickly. According to doctors, the Ben Wa balls do in fact help tighten up those muscles. However, I am still a no-go with those.

Back at the Medi Spa again, because this is where I live now, I discover a therapeutic chair that treats incontinence. It's called the BTL Emsella. This chair has a large seat, and you sit both feet on the floor with your legs hip width apart, folding forward a tad, and you just sit.

Each session is roughly thirty minutes, and it is recommended to have a series of three appointments. Oh, and you are fully clothed. I thought this was going to be quite different. I imagined vibration, and needing some alone time. Again, I was way off. Here I am sitting pretty on my chair, and I feel electric pulses through the center of my vagina all the way towards my navel: pulses and waves. Not painful, not vibration, but rather electricity. Zero sexual tingling.

The entire time I was in the chair my doctor stayed with me, and we chatted while my vagina was getting its mini workout done. I only did one session and chalked it up to market research. Even though I only did one session, it really did kickstart my Kegel strength. The day after I did feel a bit of cramping in the center of my abdomen, nothing crazy though.

I really recommend this procedure; it works. This chair is the exact type of procedure they perform for EmScuplt (the get Abs quick procedure that everyone raves about). What's good for the tummy must be good for the vagina!

## Orgasms

Remember ladies, we love these! Let's be real, we *all* love these. No need to just be a woman to love an orgasm. I have never had an issue reaching the point of orgasm several times during sex. (I am not bragging, I pinky swear). I still have no issue having them. However, they have changed. Now I typically have one instead of several. It takes longer to get there, and when it does happen, it lasts longer than in my younger years.

Not to scare anyone reading this, but did you know some women once they hit menopause cannot reach the point of an orgasm? Okay, now the cat is out of the bag. It is true. Women also dry up down there, and some of them claim sex feels like they are being stabbed, and it's incredibly painful.

## Hormones

Okay, that was a lot to unpack, and I think going through the hormones one at a time will help us. Estrogen and progesterone are not big players in the libido game; the biggest player is testosterone. While our testosterone is sky diving, so is our sex drive, and our orgasms are affected greatly. Remember I shared that mine had changed? So now that we know why, what can we do about it?

Well, as far as upping your testosterone level, you can do that through Hormone Replacement Therapy (HRT): testosterone injections, pellets, or testosterone creams. Rumor has it that the creams work very well to increase vaginal mucosa, and it helps to relieve that stabbing pain during sex. Unfortunately, creams can work better for some and not for others, depending on how their body takes to absorption.

Quick side note from my dear friend Cheri on creams that not only made me laugh my ass off but also wasn't something I had thought about. She and I were discussing menopause, and she tells me the cream is working great for her vaginal dryness and no longer has the stabbing pain during sex. Her issue is when it comes to her husband wanting to give her oral sex, she's not exactly sure what he's going to run into down there, so it's been off limits.

Let me circle back to the previous chapter when I talked about Platelet Rich Plasma (PRP). This is absolutely fascinating: the Orgasm PRP Injections. The same smarty pants that invented The PRP Facelift also invented the Orgasm PRP Injections. This gentleman, Charles Runels, MD, started looking at the orgasm system. In his research he links the brain, blood flow, and testosterone all to nerve tissue to support sex and arousal.

So here he is chilling with his girlfriend, and he has already done the face procedure on her. She's seen the results and the advantages of these procedures. This lovely lady says to him, I want you to try the PRP on my vagina. She was struggling with tightness and having difficulty reaching multiple orgasms. Again, when your plasma is injecting back into your body, your body thinks Oh! We have an injury, send in the team to repair! Your own body starts working its magic, the same way it does when you scrape your knee or cut yourself.

Dr. Wonderful says Let's do it! and agrees to do the PRP procedure on her vagina. This procedure is quite quick, around thirty minutes. Let me just quote from her what the downtime on this is like. "I can't stop masturbating! I'm still in bed! That shot made things go crazy down there!!!" According to his research and multiple other patients, this hypersexuality starts to wind down after the first week. He and she both claim she achieved increased tightness, she was more easily aroused, and her orgasms intensified.

As Dr. Wonderful saw patients, the results have been more than expected. Women are being relieved of incontinence, vaginal dryness, wimpy orgasms, and lack of desire for sex. Not to mention they've gained the advantage of increased muscle control down there. Another added goodie is that women who experience pain during sex are claiming this is all but gone after the Orgasm PRP Injection procedure.

This is such a giant breakthrough. We just don't talk enough about women's sex, especially at our age. What has happened to it in menopause? What does that mean for all of us? Emotionally, physically, and mentally. So many things suffer when our sex life is out of whack. We find it harder to connect with our partners, we have shame about it, and we experience depression. Truly this is huge! Thank you, Dr. Wonderful for caring enough about aging women to bring us such a gift.

## Rejuvenation and Reconstruction

Vaginal rejuvenation is as simple as restoring the vagina to its youthful feel and appearance. Let's dive into this, now that we have covered the orgasm shot.

Vaginal tightening can be part of a vaginal rejuvenation procedure, but it specifically tightens the vaginal canal. Women looking for this treatment are wanting to tighten up the vagina. Medically, the condition associated with this need is called vaginal laxity.

Vaginoplasty is a reconstruction of the vagina. To sum this up, it is a facelift for the inside of your vagina. Women often have this procedure when there's been a "prolapse or failure" in the pelvic floor. The surgery is minor and uses an incision and sutures under local or general anesthesia. One of my girlfriends has had this, and based on her experience it was about a five on the one to ten scale of pain. So how does it work? Your doctor removes some skin from the vaginal wall and tightens up it with stitches. Recovery time is three to four weeks. I am unsure when you can safely have sex again . . . .

Labiaplasty is a surgical procedure that trims up or reshapes the folds of skin (or vaginal lips) surrounding the vagina, called the labia minora. Childbirth and age can stretch these skin folds, so they stick out or hang below the labia. This procedure takes an hour with local anesthetic, and recovery time is also three to four weeks. Think of this one as a facelift for the outside of the vagina.

I am telling you; this is the best time to be aging! We had great music in the 90's, and now we have all these doctors while we're in our 50's figuring out how to help us have beautiful skin, keep our sex drive going, keep our precious vagina in tip-top shape, and ward off some of the severe symptoms of menopause.

> "Your best years are still ahead of you. Trust in yourself and the journey you're on." – Unknown

# CHAPTER 7

# SLEEP, BRAIN FOG, LACK OF ENERGY, MOOD SWINGS

Brain fog, boy, I remember the first time I heard this term. I was shocked it was real and linked to menopause. Honestly, I had no idea that brain fog is what was happening to me. I left my phone in the refrigerator, had increasing moments walking into rooms and not knowing why, and struggled with remembering what I told my clients I was going to accomplish for them. Even keeping track of time or keeping myself on work track was damn near impossible. If I didn't have a to-do list written down, on something I could locate easily to remind me, it was as good as gone. I even started telling my clients to call me instead of me calling them to ensure I wouldn't miss the appointment. I will absolutely forget otherwise.

So, what is the scoop with this brain fog? Estrogen. Estrogen is a key player in brain function. It influences the production of neurotransmitters, serotonin and dopamine, as well as blood flow to your brain. These are our feel-good neurotransmitters; this is why we also have mood swings during this time. Unfortunately, during all of this, lack of sleep, hot flashes, decreased sex drive, misplacing items, and trouble focusing, our bodies are under quite a bit of stress. What does a body under stress do? It elevates cortisol levels, which also causes more forgetfulness, as well as lack of sleep.

Lack of sleep at any age is naturally going to make you less sharp. According to the National Sleep Foundation, 61% of menopausal women suffer from sleep difficulties. That's a pretty big number; we are tired ladies! I have some advice below for this as well.

I do want to say that brain fog might be related to other mid-life health concerns. If you are feeling like what you are experiencing is not getting better with some of the suggestions I recommend, then you really should seek medical advice. Have your doctor check your thyroid, check for depression, and assess cardiovascular issues. You don't want to be walking around thinking it's just a symptom of menopause when it could be something very serious.

I accidentally found out that I have one of the three dementia genes by doing a DNA test for fun. I wasn't the nationality I thought I was, my brother gained a daughter, and I now sometimes worry about dementia. If you happen to fall into that category, feel free to reach out to me. I can give you some road maps on what you should be more aware of and some tests to get done early. Just because you have the dementia gene, or all three of them, doesn't mean you will get dementia.

How can we alleviate brain fog, lack of sleep and energy, and mood swings? I am going to sound like a broken record here . . . .

**1. Uplevel Your Daily Life:**

- **Healthy Diet**: Here it is again, a balanced diet. Fruits, vegetables, whole grains, lean proteins, and healthy fats support brain health. Foods high in omega-3 fatty acids, such as salmon and walnuts, are excellent.

- **Regular Exercise**: Physical activity improves blood flow to the brain and enhances mood. Both aerobic exercises and strength training do the job.

- **Sleep**: Make sleep a must, try maintaining a consistent bedtime, turn off phones, tablets and TV. Try reading a book instead or a magazine. Avoid caffeine and sugar a few hours before bedtime, and reduce alcohol intake as well. Take a hot bath or shower before bedtime. Create a calming sleep environment with a dark bedroom, and go super comfy on bedding.

**2. Stress Management**

- **Mindfulness and Meditation**: Mindfulness exercises will help reduce stress and improve focus and attention. This doesn't even require that much time commitment.

Most of us have a watch or phone that has an app for that. Shoot, even your TV has a channel for meditation. I also like to practice not giving a shit . . . .

**3. Cognitive Stimulation**

- **Mental Exercises**: Activities such as puzzles, reading, learning a new skill or language, or playing musical instruments stimulate the brain and improve your brain function. Who says you can't teach old dogs new tricks?

- **Social**: Staying socially active supports emotional and cognitive health. A good old girls' weekend, as my friend Tina says, is cheaper than therapy!

- **Laugh**: Laughing boosts your mood. Laugh at yourself, laugh with your girlfriends, laugh at life. Hopefully I have made you laugh a little while reading this book. Laughter has shown to be a powerful mood booster.

## 4. Hormone Replacement Therapy (HRT) and Supplements

- **HRT**: HRT can help alleviate brain fog symptoms by increasing your estrogen levels. Its use should be carefully considered. Have a thorough conversation with your healthcare provider and do your homework about it. HRT may have potential risks; you want to be aware of them so you can decide if this is your route. As I understand it, if you have had breast cancer in the past, HRT is absolutely something to discuss with your oncologist before you take this route.

- **Supplements**: Omega-3 fatty acids, vitamin D, and ginkgo biloba, may support brain health. These should also be discussed with your doctor, especially if you take other medication.

## 5. Professional Support

- **Go see your doctor!** See all of them. I have learned through this journey that no one cares more about my health than me. Ask questions—lots of them. Even if you are embarrassed to ask, ask. Seek out medical professionals who are not considered practitioners of "western medicine." Getting regular check-ups with your healthcare provider can help address any health conditions that are contributing to brain fog symptoms as well as all your other menopause symptoms.

- **Alternative professionals:** Acupuncture, dry needling, and yoga are good alternatives to traditional doctors and paths that may help manage and reduce stress, and have you feeling generally better.

**6. Drink Water**

- **Quantity Matters:** Just drink the water. I am not a super fan either, yet I do my very best to get in sixty to eighty ounces of water a day. Limit what you put in it as well, low sugar, low calorie, or just go straight water. If you watch these little cuties on social media videos making their fancy water and then check out the ingredients, you're basically downing a ton of sugar. Don't do that. Yes, you will pee a lot at first. You know that plant that you never water and you give it water and all the water drains immediately out? Well, that's you when you first start drinking all your water. It will subside once you get hydrated. I do really struggle with this, and I almost have to plan it out because I am just not that thirsty. I have two super cute, fun thirty-ounce bottles. I fill both up in the morning and start sucking them down the entire time I am exercising and getting ready for my day. I usually go through one by the end of the morning. My second bottle I sip on throughout the day. I typically drink one or two flavored cans of water with my meals as well. Fun fact: I bet I could suck down thirty ounces of wine with no problem. Weird, huh?!

# CHAPTER 8

# I COULD CARE LESS!

Such a dramatic shift happened in me along this journey. Was it menopause? Was it age? Was it all I have gone through in life, and I simply will no longer put up with nonsense? I have to believe it is a combination of all of those things. I have lost my desire to be a people pleaser.

I have given up on friends who require more energy than they give. I have created distance with family who don't appreciate me or what I have to emotionally offer. I have fired clients and work associates who take advantage of me, excessively take up my time, and do not value a mutually beneficial relationship. I have stopped allowing anyone to take advantage of me. I have reached my limit.

I am not upset about any of this, and when I arrived here it was peaceful, eye opening, and very freeing. I am quite happy about all of it. I do have to be honest that I have a few family relationships that still cross boundary lines, I am aware of them, and I know one day it will end. I am not perfect.

I am in the season of my life that it is all about me. I am actively striving for less to take care of. As each of my precious house plants die, I secretly get excited it is one less to water. That is how petty I have become. I want less, and I want to experience more. I want less stuff, less time-consuming activities, less work responsibilities, and less clutter around me. I found myself this year not decorating for a holiday and laughing to myself that this must be how Jehovah's Witnesses feel when everyone is getting ready for a holiday, and they are just . . . not.

One of my girlfriends is quite convincing about less house pets as well. At this point in my life, I have no idea how to live without my pets; who would I talk to? She does bring up good points though. As women, even today, we are still responsible for so much in the household, with the children, extended family, animals and more—a lot more.

Of course we have come a long way since my mother's era. Even with her, I did notice as she aged, she was no longer the homemaker she once was. I understand now. I thought she had just given up, and in sense, she had. Now I understand her focus had moved on to other things she found more intriguing in her life.

So, what's next? I may not completely have my hormones under control, and I don't know what the other side of menopause looks like. But I am in a place where I feel everything is manageable. Today I am more in touch with the relationship that I have with myself and with my husband. We have so much more life to live together, and I am looking forward to where it is all taking me and us. I strongly believe in a path, and things are meant to be. In the meantime, I have fans readily available for those unpredictable hot flashes, and I know I will get through this, just as you will. You're not alone.

I have been asked several times why I decided to write this book. It is not my chosen career and has no connection to what I do for a living. However, I have felt for a very long time that I would write a book. That feeling came with a lot of emotions about putting myself out there—not happy and exciting emotions either. I did it anyway.

When I first started going through this journey of menopause, I genuinely felt compelled to write about it. I wanted to share with other ladies what I have learned, and I wanted to make you laugh. It's just that simple.

# CHAPTER 9

# MAN-ON-PAUSE, THE OTHER SIDE OF THE STORY

### By Michael Passaglia

Ladies, let me open this chapter by saying that what I'm about to share with you is generally considered "highly confidential" and that I could lose my "man card" for being this revealing. However, in the interest of great relationships like the one I'm blessed to have and am sure many of you have as well, as well as my desire to help keep as many of those great relationships as possible on the rails through these tumultuous, confusing times, I'm willing to share some secrets. This chapter reveals truths from experiences around menopause that I'm certain you all will find illogical, so here we go!

First and foremost, you are not alone in dealing with menopause; it truly is a "couples" event. Your husband is suffering greatly and has absolutely no idea why, but he is certain that it's something that he's done differently (a.k.a wrongly). Or worse yet, he believes something has changed about him physically, romantically, attractively (think linear/visual when it comes to the male species) that causes you to no longer be the spontaneous love goddess you've always been to and for him.

We men actually "stop" our daily functions and processes and delve deeply into thought about what it could possibly be, why it has happened to us, and what we can do to fix it and get it back to where it was because obviously, we men A) Don't like change, B) Fix everything (just ask us), and most importantly, C) Don't talk about the sex we *aren't* getting because we believe it must just be happening to me.

This "stopping" phenomenon has an actual name, and ladies, I'm here to tell you that it is the root word of menopause. It's called "Man-on-

Pause." Let that sink in for a moment . . . "Menopause" = "Man-on-Pause." You see it now, right? I'm certain you feel it along with all the other "what the fuck" feelings blindsiding you as you suffer through menopause.

Menopause is incredibly cruel to the male species. I'm not asking for sympathy here, and I don't want a hot flash so stop right there if you find yourself wishing that upon me! I just want you to enjoy a "break" from your pain and suffering for a moment and live vicariously through what's left of your lovesick, tortured spouse and "walk a mile" in their shoes if you're willing to. *Hint:* You should because they love you deeply and think the now nearly non-existent "rockin" sex life is totally their fault. They believe all their buddies are sailing along getting "it" all the time like they always have since (see "C" above) guys don't talk about what they're "not" getting.

Menopause comes on quickly for the unsuspecting male. One evening we're doing what we've always done as a couple, you know, dinner date out, nice restaurant, good bottle of wine, great conversation and then home for some mutually aggressive, mutually beneficial sack romping, and then into to a deep sleep. In the blink of an eye, it becomes all of the above with a "twist." The twist being a wife who now yawns, and then falls asleep on the car ride home. Then upon arriving home she tells you, "Thank you for another wonderful evening, I love you," and then crawls into bed and falls fast asleep. By nature, men are scorekeepers, and so now wide awake in bed we begin to do the math . . . Nice dinner, "check." Good bottle of wine, "check." Good conversation, "check." And that's a wrap! The formula/equation didn't change so why did the conclusion/payout change so suddenly, and why is this now the new norm as it keeps repeating itself.

Yes ladies, we men will continue to beat our heads against the wall to see if it's just an anomaly no matter how painful. Let me tell you that when it comes to you validating your husband's manliness (or in the case of menopause, no longer validating it), participatory sex (meaning you can't just lay there and painfully, begrudgingly "take one for the team") means absolutely *everything* to your guy!

I was going to share with you what your spouse will be questioning and going through, but instead I think maybe it's better for you if I open up and share what I went through. The range of emotions is childish, humorous, and painful.

I would look at my wife snoring away in bed after a great night out that ended differently (no hot sex, no sex at all) than every other night when we did all the things prior to entering our "love nest." I'd put my hand on her, but the four-hundred-degree Fahrenheit body I touched which was also already soaking wet caused an immediate pull back. Try as I may to understand, I couldn't help but be angry and feel terribly rejected.

I saw my wife during her waking hours and daily routine still interacting with everyone as she always had: energetic, engaging, humorous, attentive, etc. It was as if nothing else had changed, only the romantic, sexual side. It's not fair, I would tell myself. I provide, I support, we travel the world together, I'm attentive, I love her, I'm attracted to her. Why is she no longer attracted to me? How can she continue to do *everything* she's always done exactly the same with the same desire and energy, but just this one thing which like it or not ladies happen to be the *most* important thing to us men (see validation comments from earlier) is the thing that's gone.

Luckily, I have an amazing wife, and we talk (and laugh) about everything. Yes, literally everything. So, she was kind enough to explain menopause and that she didn't like it either, albeit for different reasons, since she hadn't even noticed we weren't having sex anything like before. I gotta tell you to this day I laugh, and I'm sure that God has a sense of humor because he chose sex as the thing that goes away when menopause strikes. Could have chosen the desire to impulse shop . . . nope! Could have chosen spending frivolously (that way we'd only have one person out of the two of us doing that) . . . nope! Literally could have chosen *anything*, but ultimately chose sex and made it so the woman actually has no idea she's not her old self.

That's hilarious and leads to some intense conversations between man and wife and immediately puts the wife on the defensive. Let me give this a shot ladies. "You're gonna sit here and whine about the fact that I don't pole dance or strip or role play for you in our bedroom anymore while I suffer through hot flashes, brain fog and all these other "what the fuck is happening to me" feelings and try to deal with aging I don't want?" It's honestly surprising so many men have their nuts left vs. having them kicked in through conversations such as these.

I could go on and on, but my chapter is coming to an end and in trying to make it as helpful as possible I will just share a couple of thoughts. I didn't realize how far away from "us" Ang and I had gotten until she got her first "pellets." We were sitting on the couch, and we were talking as we always do, and I noticed her animation and energy towards *me*, and it dawned on me that she was her old self. I said to her "It's you! You're back." Not surprisingly, we then had spontaneous, great sex on the couch, but that's not the real point here. In retrospect I see how far we had drifted apart and how this disconnect had become our new norm and that we didn't even realize it.

I then thought about all the great relationships that have probably ended due to not understanding that menopause and "Man-on-Pause" was inserting itself and was the root of the problem. I thought about all the guys who left for younger women and laughed knowing they'd be facing this same issue not too many years from now and probably be leaving again and chalking it up to "women." I thought about all the women who must be feeling terrible about not being "young" or "vivacious" anymore even though they are still both, and their husband still adores them and longs for them.

I wondered how many great marriages just ended because neither partner knew they were actually going through the same thing together at the same time. Menopause, in my opinion, is definitely tougher on the woman, but make no mistake ladies, you're not going through it alone. The one you love most is right there next to you suffering, wondering and questioning. Talk to him, share, and hey... just a thought here... make a note (because you won't remember to spontaneously do it) to take off your top while walking through the house, and flirt with him, and tell him how much you love him! Not daily, but maybe once a week. Because no matter how shitty and unattractive you may feel, he still thinks you have the most amazing body and are the sexiest woman walking the Earth!!!

How many great marriages could have been saved if for just a little "perspective" from both sides. I know mine was, and I'm incredibly grateful.

> "You are not too old and it's not too late. You are exactly where you're meant to be."
> – Unknown

# ABOUT THE AUTHOR
# ANGELIQUEA PASSAGLIA

Angeliquea Passaglia lives with her husband and pets, splitting their time between a small town in Northern California and Nevada. She is the owner of Passaglia Insurance Agency Inc. where she has been helping businesses with group health insurance since 1997.

While she has always journaled, it was her own journey through menopause that motivated her to write *Here Comes Menopause!* As it began taking on a life of its own, she felt nudged to share it with the world . . .

Sharing her funny stories with the world doesn't come easy for Angeliquea. She's a pretty private person typically, but she knew more women needed to hear they aren't alone which is why she decided to put together and publish this book. That and the encouragement from her husband, her biggest supporter!

## More About Angeliquea

Angeliquea Passaglia began her insurance career while going to college. What started out as a job soon became a career once she fell in love with the profession. In her late twenties she established Berg Insurance Agency in Santa Maria, California. This agency specialized in Life and Health, specifically for seniors. She sold her business in 2004 to relocate to Northern California.

Once relocating to Northern California, and expanding into Northern Nevada, her focus in the insurance industry became Life Insurance as well as a huge focus on Group Health Insurance and Medicare products. She worked independently at her agency Passaglia Insurance Services, helping families obtain the much-needed coverage. "You only need to hand deliver one life insurance claim check to believe in what I do". She is incredibly passionate about this part of the industry and makes it her mission to get everyone the coverage they and their family need. She speaks to the hearts of her clients and is able to guide them easily through the process.

"I am very proud to be a part of the insurance industry, my team at Passaglia Insurance Services, Inc. is a great family, and we all have strengths to assist every aspect of our clients' insurance needs." – Angeliquea Passaglia

**Learn more at www.AngeliqueaPassaglia.com.**

# BOOK ANGELIQUEA TO SPEAK OR LEARN MORE

Angeliquea Passaglia is a very energetic and entertaining speaker. She lights up any room, event or meeting with her charm, wisdom and expertise. Plus, she makes it fun to learn more about Insurance, life's challenges and more!

You can learn more about Angeliquea and what topics she speaks on and how to book her at www.AngeliqueaPassaglia.com.

# RESOURCES

Dr. Drew on Weight loss.
https://drdrew.com/tag/weight-loss/
(accessed Dec. 27, 2024).

Harvard Health Publishing Medical School Videos.
https://www.youtube.com/@HarvardHealthPublications1/videos (accessed Dec. 27, 2024).

Runels, MD, Charles. Activate the Female Orgasm System: The Story of O-Shot®. CreateSpace Independent Publishing Platform, 2013.

Sculptra USA.
https://www.sculptrausa.com/
(accessed Dec. 27, 2024).

Verywell, Editors of Verywell Understanding Menopause. (accessed September 27, 2024).

Virpal Thiara, MD.
https://havenmedspa.com/
(accessed Dec. 27, 2024).

www.ingramcontent.com/pod-product-compliance
Lightning Source LLC
Chambersburg PA
CBHW070322100426
42743CB00011B/2520